Gaza Children Graveyard

Book 2

By: Ollie Marshall-Rico

ISBN: 979-8-89021-311-2 Paperback
ISBN: 979-8-89021-312-9 Hardback
ISBN: 979-8-89021-310-5 eBook

Printed in the United States of America

INTRODUCTION

Gaza Children Graveyard, "Book 2" is a search for inner peace within me, but unfortunately that reality has not come. A reality that refuses to come based upon the hardship and annihilation of the Palestinian people. Many sleepless nights have turned my body into knots of balls. I cry when news comes my way to say helpless babies have been left in a hospital to die alone, knowing eventually worms, maggots and flies will consume their bodies.

Netanyahu has exhibited behavior to destroy all Palestinians. Israel Military Forces, airstrikes, bombs, starvation, and Israel setters in the West Bank are key elements to reinforce Netanyahu's philosophy, that is, the goal to kill all Palestinians.

Although news media is support of Israel despite the treatment of the Palestinians, that is, the elders, the disable, the women, and the youth, which is eliminating the future of Palestinians.

There have been too many able body Palestinians' males locked up in jail for decades without reasons other than Administration Detention. Youth and females have been constantly held in jail also on Administration Detention. Israel does not have to release you once you are held on Administration Detention for years, as Israel has picked up young females. Palestinians have never been able to travel free. Their movements have always been limited from the West Bank to Gaza. It has been only allowed in medical emergencies. Regular visits with families have not been allowed.

Israel acknowledged false safety places for civilians, the hospitals, the schools, and areas of Gaza, to destroy those helpless civilians in groups one they have gathered in those places once designated as safety areas.

Prior to 1948, different religious groups lived in Palestine together. After 1948, Israel became the aggressive one to eliminate the indigenous ones of Palestine.

Israel has created a never-ending war against the Palestinians.

Never-Ending

The bullets were there for eyes to see.
Israel Military Forces killed over one hundred fathers.
Those fathers sought food for starving children.
Has the power structure become a justification for Israel killing.
The unarmed fathers were not threatening.
They only wanted food for children who needed to be fed.
This is a never-ending war that Israel continues to make possible.
Any surviving child will remember these days.

STOP COLLECTIVE PUNISHMENT
END THE SIEGE OF GAZA!
IRELAND-PALESTINE SOLIDARITY CAMPAIGN - www.ipsc.ie
SCAFHIRE

Bang, Bang, Bang, Went the Gun

Children were starving.
Fathers sought food to alleviate their children's hunger.
The sound of children's stomachs was crying out in pain.
Trucks were few, food slim picking for many.
Hands rushed for food.
The power structure is still under control.
Bang, bang, bang went the guns.
The food trucks pulled away with dead bodies all over the ground.

It Is the Death of Evil

What is this evil eye of death?
The children's stomachs ached in pain.
Their fathers waited anxiously for food delivery.
Limited food trucks finally came into play.

What is this evil eye of death?
Fathers rushed forward to claim a small quantity of food.
Food greeted their hands not.
It was the bullet guns which met the crowd of fathers.

What is this evil eye of death?
When the bullets were released, many fathers
fell to the ground.
What was that thing, to cause the death of those fathers.
Was it an evil eye dancing continually for death of all Palestinians?

What is this evil eye of death?
Is it the death of all Palestinians?
Is it the ones who dance on children's graves without a thought?
Tell me someone, so I can save these starving children.

Two Forms of Annihilation

It was a hunger style massacre **without one thought.**
Guns never stopped firing.
Helpless people stood begging to feed the children.
They are Indigenous the ones
who land was stolen many years gone.

It was a hunger style massacre without one thought.
Only the insane can enjoy such actions.
How can one steal one's land?
After which, they stomped and echoed
untruth on their graves.

It was a hunger style massacre without one thought.
Fathers stood anxiously waiting on the food trucks.
When trucks arrived, the fathers moved forward
together food.
Without a thought the IMF fired into the crowd.

It was a hunger style massacre without one thought.
Bodies fell to the ground.
Blood ran freely.
Palestinian lives and deaths are controlled
under two power structures.

Food Drops
You voted for ceasefire not.
When you voted, you were fully aware of
Palestinians starvation.
When the Palestinians gathered for food,
many were shot dead.
How do you justify the starvation of children?

A small quality of food, erase this not.
You voted for ceasefire not.
You cry and mourn as you care.
You cared not enough to vote to ceasefire.
Children continue to die with each second of a minute.
A small dropping of food, erase your vote not.
You voted for ceasefire not.
You breathe fresh air and walk freely.
Ventilation or fresh air, Palestinians have none.
They step now, knowing tomorrow or the next moment their
bodies may be splattered on the ground unrecognizable.
Your vote has spoken your thoughts.
You voted for ceasefire not.
Words do not verbalize your care stage.
Your actions go with the annihilation of the Palestinians.
You have always been aware of the conditions that the
Palestinians have been forced to indue.
I cry for the children who do you cry for this day?

Who Are You?

Who are you?
Ten babies just died from starvation.
Over one hundred fathers blood splattered on the ground
trying to obtain food.
You are still fully in support of Israel.

Who are you?
There is not any glory in your food dropping.
Your ceasefire vote would have been more appropriate.
The Palestinians people need someone to play a game of
fairness.

Who are you?
Thirteen United Nation Security Council members voted to
ceasefire.
You stood alone, no, no, ceasefire not!
What actions have you shown to stop the annihilation of the
Palestinians?

Who are you?
Israel stands strong through you.
They are killing Palestinians through your strength.
You speak at times as if you care, but your arms double-down
with Israel.

Israel is a War

Israel is at war, not Palestinians.
Israel is killing children in the name of USA.
Those children who do not die will be driven into the sea.
USA has given Israel fourteen billion dollars for the defend of
killing children.

Israel is at war, not Palestinians.
With bodies of children who are lying in the sea;
you see them not.
With bodies of children who are lying in the desert;
you see then not.
Israel is at war.

Israel is at war, not Palestinians.
With bodies of children who are lying dead from starvation,
you see them not.
Israel is at war.
With bodies of children thirsting to death,
you see them not.

Israel is at war, not Palestinians.
With bodies of children buried under debris,
you see them not.
With bodies of children walking like zombies,
you see them not.
Israel is at war.

Is there a Humane State Here?

What is less or more humane.
Killing children through airstrike or
by the bullets of the gun?
It is the state of the body when children are crying in agony
based upon unreachable food.
Children are begging for water to quest their thirst.
They are dying slowly.
When compassion is absent, the mouths of craving children
go unfed.
Where is the state of humane.

A Family Story

I often wondered why my parents huddled over me.
This day I know.
Always walk with your head in a downward motion.
Never throw a stone at the Israel Military Forces.

I often wondered why my parents huddled over me.
This day I know,
My brief lesson begins through my mother,
It was through her I learned my older sister had died as a rock
thrower.

I often wondered why my parents huddled over me.
This day I know.
Israel has all power over the Palestinians, my people.
There are not accountability acts of Israel against Palestinians.

I often wondered why my parents huddled over me.
This day I know.
Today my parents are gone with my siblings and grandparents.
I am the only one left who will look into the future
if I shall live.

Today's West Bank Kills

Gaza is in truce, West Bank not.
IMF destroyed several houses in the West Bank.
Two children died today, a nine and a fourteen-year-old.
Their lives were taken this day as others in Gaza.

Gaza is in truce, West Bank not.
IMF destroyed several houses in the West Bank.
IMF kill children without one regret.
It is an extension of their character killing
Palestinian Children.

Gaza is in truce, West Bank not.
IMF destroyed several houses in the West Bank.
They cared not about children who lived
within the houses.
The only children they see are the ones with
the cloth of Jews.

Gaza is in truce, West Bank not.
IMF destroyed several houses in the West Bank.
Children have not a life in Gaza or the West Bank.
IMF have killed children in Gaza as they continue to kill them
in the West Bank.

A Mother's Cry Nonstop

Yesterday I had five children, today I have only one.
We slept peacefully in bed.
The sound came like a thundering cloud.
Beyond that sound, there was complete silence.

Yesterday I had five children, today I have only one.
We slept peacefully in bed.
I heard not a cry from my five children.
The debris was all within my mist.

Yesterday I had five children, today I have only one.
We slept peacefully in bed.
Israel Military Forces came and demolished our home.
Why do they consider five children under
the of nine as terrorists.

Yesterday I had five children, today I have one.
We slept peacefully in bed; a sound came like a thundering
cloud.
As lightning follows thunder, my children were buried under
the debris.
I cried out, my children are buried, please help me; IMF
moved quickly down the line to continue their destruction.

What Did Truce Mean

What did truce mean?
Delayed deaths of future Palestinian children.
Children are crying begging for water.
Does anyone care for these Palestinians children?

What did truce mean?
Delayed deaths of future Palestinian Children.
Children are still begging for the necessity of life.
We are in the hands of monsters.

What did truce mean?
Delayed deaths of future Palestinian Children.
There were smiles on many faces when children
went home to Israel.
Killings continued as Administrative Detentionee were
released as Palestinians rejoiced.

What did truce mean?
Delayed deaths of future Palestinian children,
For a few days we saw the sun and walked free
until the truce ended.
Children bodies are now surrounded by me as IMF continue
to annihilate the Palestinians.

Al-Nair Hospital

Israel Military Forces forced the staff from the hospital.
Four babies were connected to breathing tubes.
They were not moveable.
IMF had one goal, empty the hospital, their guns spoke.

IMF forced the staff from the hospital.
Four babies were connected to breathing tubes.
Staff had tears in their eyes as
they were forcibly evacuated.
Leaving these babies behind, ambulance care unavailable.

IMF forced the staff from the hospital.
Four babies were connected to breathing tubes.
The staff knew the outcome of these four babies as the IMF
forced the medical personnel out.
IMF were totally in control as they forcibly
empty the hospital.

IMF forced the staff from the staff from the hospital.
Four babies were connected to breathing tubes.
Minus four babies, the hospital was emptied,
truce had come and gone.
Four babies have gone too, bugs and worms found eating on
their flush.

Slaughtered Children

Truce collapsed and Palestinians children's deaths continued.
Hamas are not killing Palestinians children.
IMF is slaughtering Palestinian's children.
Prior to the truce IMF killed over twenty thousand
Palestinians, mostly children.
Truce collapsed and Palestinians children's death continued.
Hamas are not killing Palestinians children.
Palestinians' children are being annihilated,
The annihilation is through guns, airstrike,
and necessity of food.
Truce collapsed and Palestinians children's death continued.
Hamas are not killed Palestinians children.
When children are killed, a people future siege.
Israel is killing off future generations of Palestinians.
Truce collapsed and Palestinians children death continued.
Hamas are not killing Palestinians children.
Israel has continued to killed children even in the West Bank.
The media speaks not of these children.
Truce collapsed and Palestinians children's death continued.
Hamas are not killing Palestinians children.
IMF left four babies in the hospital to slowly died.
Maggots, flies, worms festered upon newborn dead bodies.

Babies Died in Cribs

Israel glorified killing children in cribs.
The killing of Palestinians continues this day.
Israel created five thousand settler homes in the West Bank.
The settlers were issued guns to kill children
at their discretion.

Israel glorified killing children in cribs.
They see them only as causalities of war.
IMF forced the Palestinians into Southern Gaza.
As the Palestinians went to sieged South Gaza,
the killing never sieged.

Israel glorified killing children in cribs.
IMF reinforced the killing of Palestinians
by the Israel's settlers.
Babies and children held not one gun.
The media does not emphasize the killing of Palestinians.

Israel glorified killing children in cribs.
The media cry about hostages with less than two hundred
held by Hamas.
While it is speechless of thousands of Palestinian's children
being killed routinely by Israel.
Does anyone care about these children, the media speak not.

Palestinians Dying Slowly Too

Israel is killing Palestinians.
They forced Palestinians into place they are bombing.
There is not one safe place in Palestine for the Palestinians.
The home of their birth.

Israel is killing all Palestinians.
When there was a ceasefire, it helped the Palestinians not in a
lengthen period.
It was only for a brief time.
Time enough to get hostages released held by Hamas.

Israel is killing all Palestinians.
It forced them to leave Northern Gaza.
It continued to play with lives of Palestinians.
They are killing them slowly too without
the necessities of life.

Israel is killing all Palestinians.
Israel has created a strong dislike of Israel by the Palestinians,
Why should any Palestinian have a love for anyone who is
constantly killing their family members.
After destroying their home and killing their families why
would anyone expect the Palestinians to have a love for Israel.

Palestinians' children are not valuable.

Who have unequivocally condemned the killing
of children by Israel.
Why does it always have to come back to the acts of Hamas.
Israel is annihilating Palestinians' children.
Israel has been killing Palestinians' children for decades gone.
Who have unequivocally condemned the killing
of children by Israel.

Why does it always have to come back to the acts of Hama?
The West Bank Israel's settlers have been killing Palestinians'
children routinely.
If those acts were reversed, the media would
have been in uproar.
Who have unequivocally condemned the killing
of children by Israel.

Why does it always have to come back to the acts of Hamas.
All lives are valuable, Palestinians and Israel.
But the ongoing killing of Palestinians' children cannot be
compared on any level.
Who have unequivocally condemned the killing
of children by Israel.

Why does it always have to come back to the acts of Hamas?
Palestinians' children have been discarded as unevaluable.
Hamas' acts can be unacceptable,
but Israel acts are multi-worse.

Birthland Denied

Palestinians are being perished from their birthland.
Gaza residents perilous through life and death.
Wherever they are in Palestine they are not free of danger.
Every step is full of danger and risk.

Palestinians are being perished from their birthland.
Gaza residents perilous through life and death.
Israel forced Palestinians from North Gaza to South Gaza.
This was a false hope killing children in North Gaza
without justification.

Palestinians are being perished from their birthland.
Gaza residents perilous through life and death.
South Gaza they went, safe it was not.
Safe shelters had been destroyed,
leaving Palestinians in an open field.

Palestinians are being perished from their birthland.
Gaza residents perilous through life and death.
Israel desires all of Palestine,
its goal is to eliminate Palestinians.
It appears, its main goal is to kill Palestinians.

Priority Death of Children

There are two ways to eliminate the Palestinians' children.
One is to allow a slow death of starvation.
How can children survive without food or water?
The power of the IMF has been eliminating
children for decades.

There are two ways to eliminate the Palestinians' children.
One is to allow a slow death of starvation.
Children can grow up to fight for Palestine's land.
The few elders left lack the will and power to exist Israel.

There are two ways to eliminate the Palestinians' children.
One is to allow a slow death of starvation.
Palestinians' women have been viewed as weak and powerless.
Although Palestinians' women have been jailed unjustly too.

There are two ways to eliminate the Palestinians' children.
One is to allow a slow death of starvation.
Israel fears the youth who will grow into tomorrow's men.
The death of Palestinians' children has been a top
priority for Israel.

North and South Gaza

Israel has rationalized killing children with
the hunting of Hamas.
Staff with civilians were forced out of a hospital.
Four babies were left in the hospital to die.
Was Hamas hiding behind other bodies of babies.

Israel has rationalized killing children with
the hunting of Hamas.
Their parents had died in North Gaza as they had sought
safety in the hospital.
Children were fired upon in the hospital, killing many.
Children did not have one gun, but they too had
existed in South Gaza.

Israel rationalized killing children with hunting Hamas.
America power structure says Israel should kill less civilians.
Yet, it votes against UN to ceasefire in South Gaza.
Israel forced civilians out of North Gaza into South Gaza;
Palestinians' children continued to be killed.

Israel rationalized killing children with hunting Hamas.
Palestinians' children live in a total war zone.
IMF have targeted South Gaza's youth as North Gaza.
Will Israel kill all Palestinians' children before
it seeks to stop firing.

Vote or Voteless

Yesterday, you had my vote.
But, what about today?
You stand with the one who are killing children every day.
Everyday tears drop from my eyes.

Yesterday, you had my vote.
But, what about today?
I feel a sense of voteless.
I ask myself what is the purpose?

Yesterday, you had my vote.
But, what about today?
I gave my food penny to your campaign.
I took my penny back and had fish today
with my bread and gravy.

Yesterday, you had my vote.
But, what about today?
There are yellers coming into my ears, saying you must vote.
That is a crossroad unimportant to me today.

What Matters Most to You?

Is it the opinion of others or the civilians who are dying?
You speak not of the civilians who are dying by the thousands.
You have spoken the opinion of others
who cry not for the senseless killings.
Your voice should stand on its own, to speak for the helpless
ones.

What matters most to you?
Is it the opinion of others or the civilians who are dying?
Crowds have gathered to let their voices speak.
You have heard their voices; and you have spoken.
Your voice should stand on its own, to speak for the helpless
ones.

What matters most to you?
Is it the opinion of others or the civilians who are dying?
Children continue to die by the thousands.
You have spoken not to the crowds' outcry, it the popular
opinion who hold the media.
Your voice should stand on its own, to speak for the helpless
ones.

What matters most to you?
It is the opinion of others or the civilians who are dying.
There will always be opinions, one way or another.
Are you an independent thinker?
Your voice should stand on its own, to speak for the helpless
ones.

My Story.

I do not have a place to hide.
The bombs keep dropping.
The guns keep firing.
What have I done?

I do not have a place to hide.
The bombs keep coming.
The guns keep firing,
A mother with a child lies dead over yonder.

I do not have a place to hide.
The bombs keep coming.
The guns keep firing.
A teen covered his body over his baby sister,
both now, lay breathless.

I do not have a place to hide.
The bombs keep coming.
The guns keep firing.
Will anyone be left to tell our story?

I Find It Not

Security space, where may I find it?
I have not a space in my heart to cry for any hostages.
My entire family has been annihilated.
This is my story.

Security space, where may I find it?
I have not a space in my heart to cry for any hostages.
I have seen children less aged than I with dismantled head
from their bodies.

Security space, where may I find it?
I have not a space in my heart to cry for any hostages.
I will take you to a safer place, South Gaza, said my mother.
My mother died in South Gaza trying to reserve my life.

Security space, where may I find it?
I have not a space in my heart to cry for any hostages.
My mother died huddling me within her arms.
This is my story.

Aid Not Deliverable

Aid is not reasonable deliverable.
The children keep dying,
The power structure says kill less civilians.
Yet, it supports the killing of civilians with its each action.
How many civilians will live to retell future generations?

Aid is not reasonable deliverable.
The children keep dying.
When children are not annihilated completely, their thoughts
will lie where?
Will they thank Israel for not killing them while their family
members are dead.
How many times will they relive Israel
annihilating their family?

Aid is not reasonable deliverable.
The children keep dying.
Will the few surviving children think of how
their siblings died?
Or will they know Israel killed them either through
starvation, bombing or guns.
Will there be a created wall of hate built upon Israel's actions?

Aid is not reasonable deliverable.
The children keep dying.
Will the few surviving children know why they have land not?
Will they know Israel lives on their ancestors' land, Palestine?
Will there be another name as Hamas?

False Safety

Israel goal is to eliminate the Palestinians.
It includes Gaza and the West Bank too.
Israel Military Forces never police its own settlers
in the West Bank.
Israel's settlers have constantly violated Palestinians' civilians.
It is not antisemitic to oppose the lack of
humanitarian acts of Israel.

Israel goal is to eliminate the Palestinians.
Israel's settlers are the only ones who have guns.
They have constantly shot Palestinians.
Palestinians were always forbidden to travel freely from Gaza
to the West Bank.
It is not antisemitic to oppose the lack of
the humanitarian acts of Israel.

Israel goal is to eliminate the Palestinians.
Israel has treated the Palestinians less than worse stepchildren.
Only under urgent medical cases they were allowed
to travel from Gaza.
How can one not understand a growing dislike for Israel.
It is not antisemitic to oppose the lack of
the humanitarian acts of Israel.

Israel goal is to eliminate the Palestinians.
It forced the Palestinians into Southern Gaza for false safety.
After which, it made several airstrikes into Southern Gaza.
Israel had already bombed South Gaza prior to sending
Palestinians there.
It is not antisemitic to oppose humanitarian acts of Israel.

Traveling to Death

The evacuation from North Gaza to South Gaza
was a death trap.
Palestinians have water not.
They have food not.
They are surrounded in despair with misery.

The evacuation from North Gaza to South Gaza
was a death trap.
Palestinians dropped dead based upon lack of necessities.
Children walking aimlessly.
Parents are unable to respond to their children's needs.

The evacuation from North Gaza to South Gaza
was a death trap.
One of two last siblings died without comfort.
Airstrikes and bombs had taken five other siblings
with their parents.
Silent tears roll down the cheeks of the last sibling.

The evacuation from North Gaza to South Gaza
was a death trap.
Destination completed, where are the resources?
South Gaza is not a place where one's head can peacefully rest.
The endlessly goal here is death in the end.

Southern Gaza

Bullets and bombs have taken lives here too.
Israel told us a false reality go southern to be safe.
In a father's arms a two-year-old died from starvation.
A sixteen-year-old girl is paralyzed for life.
Yes, bullets and bombs have taken Palestinians
lives in South Gaza.

Bullets and bombs have taken lives here too.
The protector's father is I deep agony.
He lacks the power to save a child he brought forth to life.
He knows the Israel's monster who has brought this to be.
The one who defines Palestinians as pigs
in pins to be slaughtered,
Bullets and bombs have taken lives here too.
A bomb has moved the mobility from a sixteen-year-old.
A paralyzed body does not function with a genius mind.
Her entire family gone, under the debris
that left her in this state,

Hope, she has not, Israel has stolen and denied her the
necessity of life and her mobility.
Bullets and bombs have taken lives here too.
They forced us into Southern Gaza, killing us still.
Parents are trying to put smiles on little ones' eyes.
But those eyes are not in a naïve state.
Their stomachs feel the pain lacking the necessities of life.

Ceasefire Not

Israel Military Forces bombed where they please.
They have bombed children's schools.
They have consciously selected not to bomb
the West Bank Palestinians.
Since Israel's settlers have guns to kill Palestinians at will,
support with IMF.

Israel Military Forces bombed where they please.
The Big Power One supported ceasefire not.
The children have become casualties of the war.
Safety corroders have been bombed.

Israel Military Forces bombed where they please.
Palestinians left North Gaza and went to
South Gaza for safety.
When Palestinians reached South Gaza, they were bombed.
Palestinians were confused with South Gaza devastation.

Israel Military Forces bombed where they please.
Families live in open streets without shelter.
Food is not to be found in the mouths of children.
Starvation, bombs, and airstrikes have claimed many
children's lives within South Gaza.

These are the results of the United Nation Security Council Vote on Ceasefire as follows.

USA was the only country to vote no for ceasefire not to begin in Gaza.

1. Algeria---------------------Yes

2. USA-------------------------No

3. Russian Federation-------Yes

4. China-----------------------Yes

5. Slovenia--------------------Yes

6. Switzerland----------------Yes

7. France----------------------Yes

8. Mozambique----------------Yes

9. Republic of Korea----------Yes

10. Japan-----------------------Yes

11. Malta------------------------Yes

12. United Kingdom-----------Abstain

13. Sierra Leone----------------Yes

14. Ecuador---------------------Yes

15. Guyana----------------------Yes

The United Nation Security Council should protect those who are not able to protect themselves as the Palestinians. The only country that voted no was the USA. Children are being murdered without anyone coming to their aid.

Al-Fakhoura School

Israel airstrikes another safe shelter.
Women and baby bodies were spread throughout the floor.
Israel military power is supported by the Big Power One.
There has been absolutely a lack of concern when bombs
splattered children's bodies.

Israel airstrikes another safe shelter.
There was a deadly impact on the children from the airstrike.
The horrifying incident killing children with this airstrike
have escaped their mind.
These children were viewed as animals because of their
Palestinians background.
Israel airstrikes another safe shelter.
Blooded bodies of children are splattered
throughout the room.
Unidentifiable to many, their bodies were mashed
as ground beef.
Israel has demolished UN Shelters which have been viewed as
safety nets for children and women.

Israel airstrikes another sate shelter.
Jabalya City Shelter was splatter into pieces, killing children.
Israel has continued its genocide without
the thought of children.
Who would think that Israel would bomb UN shelters?

Babies Arrived Critically

Thirty-six were expected, twenty-six arrived.
Birth through cell light, electricity none.
Compacted to survive, many could not linger.
Airstrikes and bombs have taken away the baby's mother.

Thirty-six were expected, twenty-six arrived.
Four mothers with six nurses journey the enroute trip.
Twenty-two babies have been orphan through Israel' s bombs.
Israel killed their mothers.

Thirty-six were expected, twenty-six arrived.
Will a community member pass on their family's legacy?
The comfort of their mother will never be felt.
Hopefully, someone will tell them the story if Israel does not
kill them prior.

Thirty-six were expected, twenty-six arrived.
Israel killed several babies.
They took away the necessity of life.
Medical care was denied, babies who could not linger died.

Humanitarian Crisis

Israel cried terrorists with the capitol of
two hundred civilians.
With the support fully of the USA President Biden.
Each cried loudly for hostages
who had been taken at a concert.
Both, Israel, and the USA President, yelled the name Hamas.

Israel cried terrorists with the capitol of
two hundred civilians.
With the support fully of the USA President, Biden.
Each looked at this event in isolation.
Netanyahu, spoke not of unjustified killing of Palestinians.

Israel cried terrorists with the capitol of
two hundred civilians.
With the support fully of the USA President Biden.
Each looked not at thousands of Palestinians jailed previously
unjustifiably by Israel, the media cried not.
Children and women of two hundred civilians were held by
Hamas and the media cried out.

The Platform

Where are the purest people?
Are there any on this road?
Are they true believers?
Who are the creators of the story?
Are there any deceptions within their lines?
When they harm someone will it come back on them?
Have they created the story to support their point of view?

What is the hidden agenda?
Will things return to them when they throw punches?
Will all receive justice in the end?
Those who are genuine can correct themselves
when they stumble.
They should know their heart for pureness.
Their hearts should be able to stand with
the noble causes on earth.
When they look to correct others, it is done softly.
Have they been carefully with words chosen.
Will another siege upon what they say or do?
When the wind blows from the tree,
will they breathe in the air?
Let those who speak from the platform be truthful.

The Killers

Israel, you bombed the schools.
Without a thought, Israel proved its strength,
it killed children.
Just for throwing rocks they have put children
in prison for years.
Who would have known if Hamas pen-up emotions
had not exploded.
Israel, you bombed the schools.
Media complained of hostages takes by Hamas.
Israel jails are filled with children and women of Palestinians.
Many would not have known if Hamas

if Hamas had not acted.
Israel, you bombed the schools.
Media has not room to complain about Nazi upon Jews.
Israel is not a defense force, they are military forces,
created to kill Palestinians.
We would not have known if Hamas had not acted, but for
those who died at the concert I cry too.
Israel, you bombed the schools.
The lives lost and the hostages that were taken at the concert
have saddened me.
But not greater than the murdered children killed
continually by Israel.
Only through Hamas action, we have learned
the cruelness of Israel.

Palestine Truth

What is the truth about Palestine?
Israel has seized it and has total control.
The civilians' homes Israel attacked upon
its own destructions.
The freedom of children has existed not under Israel.

What is the truth about Palestine?
Israel has seized it and has total control.
Israel is seeking the remaining land of the Palestinians.
Palestinians live as prisoners on this land controlled by Israel.

What is the truth about Palestine?
Israel has seized it and has total control.
Israel has never honored the Palestinians rights to exist.
As Netanyahu has said several times, they are animals.

What is the truth about Palestine?
Israel has seized it and has total control.
Palestinians never experienced a normal life in Gaza or the
West Bank.
Their homes, land, freedom, and rights are total
under control by Israel.

Orphans

Your truth has not been the death of children.
The death of Children in Gaza is in a state of genocide.
These children do not have guns.
Many have not reached the first year of birth.
Many is this, other than genocide?
Your truth has not been the death of children.
When one will sing the children truth of Gaza,
it will not be antisemitic.
Labor it antisemitic if you wish,
Israel is still murdering children.
One can ache for Palestinians' children,
without being antisemitic.
Palestinians' children have been locked up for years
without the media crying out.

Your truth has not been the death of children.
Palestinians' children should be held with care,
without the necessities of life.
Children who have not been military killed,
have been put in a state of starvation.
How would one define this state, other than genocide.
The Brutality of Gaza's children has continued
without stopping.
Your truth has not been the death of children.
Premature babies have died when Israel denied their care.
Israel has placed children in concentration for many years.
Many children have become orphans
who have not died in Gaza.
Children stood in the mist of debris
when their entire family died.

Is Hope for the Palestinians?

Is there hope for the Palestinians?
Those who have lingered in prison without a cause for years.
Those who have lived openly in concentration campus.
Under the supervision of Israel, with every move dictated.

Is there hope for the Palestinians?
Israel calls Hamas terrorists.
What are terrorists?
Will Israel and Hamas both acts be identified as terrorist ones.
Israel acts are killing children, defensibly ones.

Is there hope for the Palestinians?
For four decades, Israel has held children in jail.
Who have grown-up now to be men behind bars.
Israel calls Hamas terrorists.
Israel turns children into ground beef in the mist of debris.

Is there hope for the Palestinians?
With the killing of premature babies, it appears not.
Israel has tightened the rope around the Palestinians' necks.
Was this rope twisted too tightly to create October 7, 2023?
Is there hope for the Palestinians after mostly thirty thousand
women and children having been slaughtered by Israel?

Waiting Anxiously

Families waited anxiously for their loved ones.
It has been short of two months, but years in mind.
Families hold up pictures and detail their relationship.
They bite their tongues not, denouncing Hamas as a terrorist.

Families waited anxiously for their loved ones.
This has been an endlessly period for the Palestinians.
Many decades years have come and gone.
Without a bit of hope over seeing their loved ones, who had
been taken by Israel years gone.

Families waited anxiously for their loved ones.
It had been short of two months, but yeas in mind.
An agreement had been reached for some to return
to their families.
Less than two hundred hostages or more were still
held by Hamas.
Families waited anxiously for their loved ones.
Over eight thousand Palestinians have been forced
into Israel prison.
Palestinians' families have lost hope in ever seeing
their loved ones.
There is a lack of media telling their stories,
double children standard.

A Disconnected Child

A child was in shock.
Debris surrounded him.
He saw a soul not.
Where is his family?

A child was in shock.
He went to bed with his family.
He does not see his siblings.
Where are his parents?

A child was in shock.
He looked around.
He saw not a soul but heard the distant cry of another child.
He followed the sound and found it buried under debris.

A child was in shock.
He tried to open his mouth as he heard the echo of his sound.
His mouth was closed shut.
He stood there with tears rolling silently down his cheeks.

Temporary Truce to Stop Killing

Hamas paid Israel to stop murdering children temporary.
It was called A Truce, as Israel received some hostages.
This truce allowed the children to breathe and see
the sun for a few days.
A convoy of trucks lined up with food to enter Gaza.
Water and food had hoped to enter Gaza to feed
the starving children.
Hamas paid Israel to stop murdering children temporary.
It was called truce, as Israel received some hostages.
This truce was the shortest finger on one's hand.
Did water and food enter Gaza to feed all
the starving children?

Hamas paid Israel to stop murdering children temporary.
It was called A Truce, as Israel received some hostages.
The children did not hear or feel the bombs for a few days.
It is said Israel is trying to eradicate the Palestinians' future
through the children.
Hamas paid Israel to stop murdering children temporary.
It was called A Truce, as Israel received some hostages.
For a few days, the children received fresh water.
Without fear of losing their lives,
they walked in the sun freely.

An Illusion

An evacuation to South Gaza was an illusion for safety.
Bombs were dropping throughout Gaza.
Children, women, and the elders' lives
were taken without mercy.
Does anyone care for the annihilation of the Palestinians.

An evacuation to South Haza was an illusion for safety.
Palestinians were forced out of North Gaza
under the threat of death.
Annihilation of the Palestinian Group is in full force.
Israel is killing Palestinians as a tsunami sweeps
everything in its site.
An evacuation to South Gaza was an illusion for safety.
The elders are crying like children without hope.
The elders cry for the pain they see in the eyes of the children.
The elders have seen many stages on the treatment with the
Palestinians' people from Israel.

An evacuation to South Gaza was an illusion for safety.
Does anyone care in the world that children
are brutally being killed?
People with power lips are silent, they speak not.
The silent does speak, they are only Palestinian's children.

Generations Wiped Out

Generations have been wiped out totally.
From grandparents to infants, families are gone.
Grieving Palestinians want to know why.
Israel wants Gaza Strip uninhabitable;
its hidden agenda is for the land.

Generations have been wiped out totally.
From grandparents to infants, families are gone.
Every area in the Gaza Strip has been bombed.
Safe places are none, hospital wards have been destroyed.
Generations have been wiped out totally.
From grandparents to infants, families are gone.
The besieged of the Gaza Strip,
Israel Military Forces faces grinned deeply.

The power of Israel Military Forces,
wipe out generations of children with pride.
Generations have been wiped out totally.
From generations to infants, families are gone.
Children who have yet to be killed, wait anxiously in the wind
hoping for that day not to come.
Shelter, food, water, and the comfort of loved ones are
incomprehensible.

Children on Two Sides

When Israel Military Forces begin again their children
will be safe after the truce.
Palestinians' children will be facing death.
It will be either by bombs, airstrikes or by starvation.
Israel's children will have a bed to rest their heads.
When Israel Military Forces begin again their children
will be safe after the truce.

Palestinians' children will be facing death.
A home they will not have,
debris with family members beneath.
It is a sad world for the Palestinians, this is not a celebration.
When Israel Military Forces begin again their children
will be safe after the truce.

Palestinians' children will be facing death.
Open air will be their home, not shelter to shield
the coldness from their body.
Children released for uncommitted crimes,
the world cried or song not.
When Israel Military Forces begin again their children
will be safe after the truce.

Palestinians' children will be facing death.
An understanding counseling will be available
for Israel's children.
Most Israel's children will walk their lives back into normality.

Killings Connected

Israel is killing Palestinians as Nazil killed Jews.
Except Israel kills are mostly children.
Many are shouting, unbelievable, continue the kills.
Debris holds buried bodies this day as it will tomorrow.

Israel is killing Palestinians as Nazi killed Jews.
Except Israel kills are mostly children.
Today was a truce day, but tomorrow will come again.
Release today's Palestinians will be among tomorrow's debris.

Israel is killing Palestinians as Nazi killed Jews.
Except Israel kills are mostly children.
Children have died on several levels.
Starvation, bombs, and ling airstrikes have claimed
numerous children's lives.

Israel is killing Palestinians as Bazi killed Jews.
Except Israel kills are mostly children.
Israel has a hidden agenda for Gaza and the West Bank.
That agenda does not include a statehood for the Palestinians.

Israel Military Forces

Israel Military Forces teargassed two children
as they gathered happily.
Anticipated family released from years of jail
came with smiles.
IMF released teargas upon this crowd,
bringing down two children.
An act, unnecessary, other than a show of military power.

IMF teargassed two children as they gathered happily.
Those children were not a threat to Israel's population.
It was simply a show of aggression upon those children.
The type of aggression that had previously jailed so many
Palestinians' children.
IMF teargassed two children dimming their hope,
Palestinians have not been allowed to be children
under Israel's rule.
A child has thrown a rock at an Israel person and has been
locked up for decades.
A young woman was locked up for just having a knife.

IMF have rules not when it comes to Palestinians' children.
They have killed and put children in jail for decades
without a cause.
Israel call Hamas terrorists, but what define them as not
terrorists against the Palestinian' community.
To understand the mildew behind the walls,
look for the water.

Hamas Defense

Hamas has been considered a line of defense for Palestinians.
Palestinians elected Hamas as their representatives.
Bush at that time was the President of the USA.
Israel and the USA interfered with the election results.

Hamas has been considered a line of defense for Palestinians.
Jews first went into a mosque and killed
forty-one people with a bomb.
After that act, Hamas decided to return
that form of aggression.
Israel never accepted Hamas' election,
although they were chosen fairy.

Hamas has been considered a line of defense for Palestinians.
When they were elected, Israel blocked all Gaza's necessities.
Good and supplies in Gaza continued to be control by Israel.
Israel did not credited Hamas with the ability to rule when
they were selected to rule by the people.

Hamas has been considered a line of defense for Palestinians.
Israel has attempted to completely
dehumanized the Palestinians.
Israel have had complete control of the Palestinians' lives since
they moved into Palestine in 1948.
Gaza and the West Bank Palestinians have not been able to
make decision centered around their lives.

Hamas has been considered a line of defense for Palestinians.
When Palestinians have left any location in Palestine, most
times they have been forbidden to return to their homes
occupied previously.

Since Israel's recent war, many Palestinians tried to return to
North Gaza, just to try and bury their dead; IMF shot two
males dead as they attempted that journey,
when the first truce was in place.
Hamas has been considered a line of defense for Palestinians.
They have supplied only the necessity for the Palestinians
with limited power.
Israel has never allowed Hamas to rule Gaza as elected.
That itself was much too close for statehood.

Hamas has been considered a line of defense for Palestinians.
Once Israel told Palestinians to leave their homes for ten days.
When Palestinians sought to return in ten days within that
location, Israel barred them out.
Israel has always had it eyes on all of Palestine land.

Hamas has been considered a line of defense for Palestinians.
Israel forced Palestinians out of North Gaza.
IMF killed individuals who tried to return to bury loved ones.
Gaza is another place Israel looks to occupy from the
Palestinians.

Hamas has been a line of defense for Palestinians.
When Israel took control of the line it occupies currently it
jailed thousands of Palestinians.
Throughout the years it has continued to jail Palestinians.
Israel holds many Palestinians on Administration Detention
for years without supplying a reason.

Hamas has been considered a line of defense
for the Palestinians.
Palestinians' teenagers are judged
in a two-tiered justice system.
Palestinians' teenagers are killed and locked up
for years for throwing rocks.
Israel's teenagers have never faced any charges
for throwing rocks.

Hamas has been considered a line of defense
for the Palestinians.
When there were disputes in the community,
Hamas was able to control it.
The youth have viewed Hamas as a positive force
in the community.
This attitude has been based upon the treatment the youth has
received from IMF and the Israel's settlers.

Hamas has been considered a line of defense
for the Palestinians.
Since Israel has occupied Palestine,
more Palestinians die every year.
Over 30,000 Palestinians have died this year where
appropriately 1400 Israeli have died.
The majority of the 30,000 Palestinians
who have died were children.
Hamas has been considered a line of defense
for the Palestinians.
Palestinians are nomad forced to move from place to another.
Real nomads have freedom to move as choice, but it has been
forced upon the Palestinians.
Israel cannot kill all Hamas unless they are prepared to kill
most of the Palestinians.

Hamas is considered a line of defense for the Palestinians.
Israel refused to uphold its agreement with certain
prisoners' release.
Those release should have never been jailed;
a crime never was committed.
Israel has refused to release prisoners who have been held for
decades without a cause.

A Student Removed from Campus

A student, Arzel Muhammad, was kicked off campus.
She was a Palestinian's student.
She defined herself as Anti-Zionist, not antisemitic.
She called the action of Israel Military Forces
as behavioral of Nazi.
She included those who support
the killing of children as Nazi too.
Where do I stand?
Israel Military Forces are killing indefensible children.
If this is not a form of Nazi behavior, what is it?
This is the worse type of killing.
Killing children to serve one's purpose.
Children who are still feeding on their mothers' breath.
One cannot justify killing children on any level.
Israel has an underlining purpose.

The Nazi wanted to obliviate the Jews.
Israel action is ending future generations of Palestinians by
killing of babies and children.
Israel students were expressing their opinion
by supporting the action of Israel.
It was correct for this Palestinian's student to express her
opinion as it was for the Israel's students.

A campus is a place to express various ides of opinions.
Unfortunately, the media and USA are overly supportive of
Jews and are willing to deny other their rights,
such as the Palestinians.
Jews are extremely powerful in the USA, which means at
times, other people rights may be ignored.
People are immediately classified as antisemitic when they do
not agree with Zionist ideas.

Over Forty-Years Gone

Genocide of the Palestinians have occurred through Israel.
Israel has imprisoned some Palestinians over forty years.
These imprisoned Palestinians do not have any rights.
Many have been beaten at Israel will.
They die in prison without proper medical care.

Genocide of the Palestinians have occurred though Israel.
Israel has imprisoned some Palestinians over forty years.
Israel has denied them contact with
their family members in prison.
When imprisoned Palestinians have died,
families have gone unnotified.
They have died in prison without adequate food.

Genocide of the Palestinians have occurred through Israel.
Israel has imprisoned some Palestinians over forty years.
They picked up children and women
and have imprisoned them at will.
Israel has placed many Palestinians in jail on
Administration Detention.
Administration Detention means it is at Israel discretions.

Genocide of the Palestinians have occurred through Israel.
Israel has imprisoned some Palestinians over forty-years.
IMF hold Palestinians behind bars
for years without an explanation.
IMF have used Palestinians as shooting targets
at their discretion.

The Eyes of God

All lives are precious in the eyes of God.
Those lives who were taken by Hamas.
Their families have suffered and cried.
Children, women, and men were killed.
Their families yelled out for the hostages taken that day.

All lives are precious in the eyes of God.
Palestinians' lives who have been shot daily by Israel.
Their families have suffered and cried too with media silence.
Children and women, are killed,
go without public notification.
They are never called hostages; they are called terrorists.

All lives are precious in the eyes of God.
Returned Israel's hostages, families were overly rejoiced.
The public was pleased.
Explanation is not needed here; the people know
why they were taken.
One may not agree with Hamas' method, but the suffering of
the Palestinians was brought before all eyes of the people.

All lives are precious in the eyes of God.
Beyond comprehension, Palestinians are appropriating over
thirty thousand deaths with civilians.
Israel authority has described civilians as animals and treated
them in that manner.
Israel had selectively chosen to limit its killings when the
truce was in action.
Netanyahu has dictated people's orders in Israel when it has
come to the Palestinians as other prior leaders.

Is It Unfair?

People talk about Israel's hostages returning home.
They speak not of thousands of Palestinians
who are still in jail.
Does anyone care about those Palestinians?
Have the Palestinians been exiled in their birthland?

People talk about Israel's hostages returning home.
They speak not of thousands of Palestinians
who are still in jail.
Too many jailed, just by holding the name as a Palestinian.
Where is the fairness of all that madness?

People talk about Israel's hostages returning home.
They speak not of thousands of Palestinians
who are still in jail.
Too many years gone, families have died with lost connection.
Families connected burial not, just Palestinians' deaths.

People talk about Israel's hostages returning home.
They speak not of thousands of Palestinians
who are still in jail.
I cry, their families cry too.
We all cry for the sadness it holds.

Over Thirty Thousand Dead

Over thirty thousand gone and the bombs
keep dropping non-stop.
How did Palestinians with homes become nomads within
their land?
Are they viewed as slaves by Netanyahu?
Babies and all are casualties of his war, they hold not the
lowest class as a slave.

Over thirty thousand gone and the bombs
keep dropping non-stop.
The new nomads have not a place to seek total security.
They go south seeking safety and find it not.
The game of security with Israel pulling
the cards does not exist.

Over thirty thousand gone and the bombs
keep dropping non-step.
They are in an open field without food, water, or shelter.
Children are dying by the thousands
in the arms of loved ones.
Their parents are helpless; Israel has all the power.

Over thirty thousand gone and the bombs
keeps dropping non-stop.
They are Palestinians without Palestine.
Israel has taken control of Palestine, and it is moving to
annihilate the Palestinians.
Many Palestinians are wondering around as zombies within
their lost land.

Rucksacks

Frantically, they gathered their belongings in rucksacks.
Israel Military Forces had attacked another, Hospital, Nassar.
Civilians continues to die, holders of the Palestinians' name.
Israel, safety zone previously, Khan Younis had become
another Netanyahu' contradiction.

Frantically, they gathered their belongings in rucksacks.
ISF have taken over the hospital.
Several youths lost their lives on this day.
IMF bulldozer destroyed the hospital perimeter wall.

Frantically, they gathered their belongings in rucksacks.
Those not killed here, where will they flee now?
Every designated safety zone has been uprooted through IMF.
Palestinians are nomads fleeing to fine some form
of a safety zone.

Frantically, they gathered their belongings in rucksacks.
Despair runs through their bones,
To stay in the hospital these civilians would have
to confront the IMF.
When they left the hospital, the Palestinians were entering
into apocalyptic landscape,

Job Completed

When Israel eliminates all Palestinians,
Netanyahu job will be completed.
It will include unborn babies who have not seen daylight.
The babies who are pushing their mothers' stomachs outward.
These are just babies who are Netanyahu's casualties of war.

When Israel eliminates all Palestinians,
Netanyahu job will be completed.
Hospitals and school shelters have been eliminated, based
upon their destruction.
The despair of Palestinians affects not their lives for survival.
Children dying of starvation.

When Israel eliminates all Palestinians,
Netanyahu job will be completed.
The Palestinians cry of survival, mean nothing to Netanyahu.
Netanyahu pushes on all levels to eliminate the Palestinians.
He cherishes the observation of mothers watching their
children die of starvation.

When Israel eliminated all Palestinians,
Netanyahu job will be completed.
He seeks to drive Palestinians into the desert and sea.
He cherishes over the suffering
and dying starvation of the children.
Netanyahu's goal is to obtain additional land to add to the
stolen land taken in 1948.

Starvation

Starvation has casted a shadow over Ramadan.
Over twenty-five people have died based upon starvation.
Israel is seeking to jail thousands of Palestinians who have not
starved to death or have been killed with bombs and guns.
IMF have prevented Palestinians who wish to honor Ramadan
by beating them away from the building with sticks.
Jewish Israelis care not for Palestinians.

They want Netanyahu to kill the Palestinians
who are in Rafah.
The people in Rafah have already been displaced several times.
Rafan is the southernmost city of Gaza.
Netanyahu told Palestinians to leave north Gaza
to go south for safety.
Netanyahu goal is to annihilate Palestinians
without a viable justification.
Palestinians want to be free of dying by Israel.

Forbidden the Practice of Ramadan

Palestinians are not able to practice Ramadan.
They cannot abstain from food of their own choice.
Because Israel has denied food intake through starvation.
Israel has not permitted the availability of clear water.
Netanyahu knows the important of Ramadan to Palestinians
He cares not.

Ramadan Denied

Ramadan calls for a month of fasting from sunrise to sunset.
It calls for a deep reflection upon one's life.
It deals with spirituality within one's soul.
Palestinians who practice these steps cultivate a better
relationship with their God.

Ramadan calls for a month of fasting from sunrise to sunset.
Netanyahu has chosen not to honor a ceasefire, dishonoring
Ramadan's worshipers.
Surprise not, it stands, it is the Muslim way of life.
Netanyahu has denied all life support for Palestinians,
taking away food.

Ramadan calls for a month of fasting from sunrise to sunset,
Food, water, and fuel have left thousands of Palestinian dead.
Starvation is the worse form of a weapon.
Palestinians who attempted to worship in the Holy Temple
were met with weapons.

Ramadan calls for a month of fasting from sunrise to sunset.
Muslims do not have to abstain from eating
from sunrise to sunset.
Because Netanyahu has stolen this chosen in Gaza.
Will anyone come to the Palestinians rescue, the children,
the women and the elders?